Military Aircraft Library
Research Planes

Military Aircraft Library
Research Planes

DR. DAVID BAKER

Rourke Enterprises, Inc.
Vero Beach, FL 32964

RESEARCH PLANES

The NASA HiMAT research plane drops away from its Boeing B-52 carrier plane at the start of a powered test flight.

Library of Congress Cataloging-in-Publication Data

Baker, David, 1944-
  Research planes.

  (Military aircraft library)
  Includes index.
  Summary: Discusses how new designs and innovations are researched, tested, and incorporated into the production of fighter planes.
  1. Airplanes, Military—United States—Juvenile literature. [1. Airplanes, Military] I. Title.
II. Series: Baker, David, 1944-   . Military planes.
UG1243.B34 1987   358.4'183'0973   87-3355
ISBN 0-86592-354-X   623.746

CONTENTS

The Search for Speed

No airplane anywhere in the world had achieved supersonic speed in level flight until the X-1 series in the 1940s, seen here being tailed by an F-86 Sabre fighter.

Supersonic airplanes are a familiar sight in the sky and have been for many years. There was a time, however, when most people thought the speed of sound might be an impenetrable barrier beyond which flight would be impossible. The Wright brothers are credited with having made the world's first powered flight of a heavier-than-air flying machine in December, 1903. Slow technical progress was made over the next few years. In 1917, the National Advisory Committee for Aeronautics (NACA) was formed to conduct research on the science of flight and flying. By the mid-1940s, military airplanes were flying at nearly 500 MPH in level flight and almost 600 MPH in a dive. Scientists knew they were getting close to the speed of

sound where strange things happened. Planes were severly buffeted, sometimes to destruction, as air particles were squeezed to form what seemed like a barrier.

The speed of sound is about 760 MPH at sea level. It decreases slowly as the temperature of the air decreases, and the temperature of the air drops as altitude increases. At an altitude of 36,000 feet, the speed of sound is only 660 MPH. It remains at this level all the way up to the maximum height at which an airplane can fly. Because a plane needs a lift, there is a limit to how thin the air can be before a plane loses stability. Although different for specific designs, the limit is usually considered to be around 100,000 feet, or about 19 miles.

The Bell X-1 made the world's first recorded supersonic flight in October 1947 and for several years proved invaluable as a high-speed research plane.

In 1944, Congress provided funds for the NACA to conduct research on this strange barrier and to build a plane that could push against what some people called the "sonic wall." Officially this barrier was known as *Mach 1*, after the mathematician Ernst Mach who first defined the laws of supersonic speed. Because the United States was at war with Germany and Japan, the work went ahead in great secret. Several airplane companies proposed different designs, but Bell was chosen to build what is now called the X-1. First in a long line of X-series research aircraft, the X-l was ready to fly by January, 1946.

Wheels down, the X-1 comes in to a smooth landing after a test flight. Note the square shaped side hatch through which the pilot gets in and out of the cockpit and the streamlined nose incorporating a flat windshield.

The X-1 series is powered by a single rocket motor consisting of four chambers, any one or combination of which could be ignited for flight after release from a carrier plane.

The Bell X-1 was unlike any other plane before it. Conventional propeller-driven designs were incapable of pushing anything through the sound barrier, so a rocket motor was chosen. Because motors burn fuel very quickly, its 6,000 pounds of thrust would last just 5 minutes, not enough time for the X-1 to get off the ground and accelerate to supersonic speed. So the tiny X-1 weighing just 6 tons, would be carried into the air under the fuselage of a converted B-29 bomber. The X-1 was only 31 feet long with a wingspan of 28 feet. It took its design from the shape of a .50 caliber bullet.

Three X-1 planes were built, but the third was destroyed in a fire before flight. The first two were used in an extensive sequence of 49 tests in which the research plane was carried into the air beneath the B-29 and, on some occasions, dropped for a glide back down to the ground. Over a period of time, there were eight powered flights with the first X-1 and six with the second. Slowly, speed had been built up to just short of Mach 1. Finally, on October 14, 1947, Major Charles (Chuck) Yeager strapped himself into the first X-1 and prepared for the world's first supersonic flight.

It was about 10:00 A.M. when the laden bomber roared into the air. Twenty minutes

Modified to incorporate a canopy over the cockpit through which the pilot could gain access, several changes and improvements were made to the X-1B as the test program went along.

later, at a height of 20,000 feet, the bright orange Bell X-1 fell away. Seconds later, Yeager ignited two of the four chambers on the rocket motor and felt acceleration as he rocketed toward 40,000 feet. Leveling off, he lit a third burner on the rocket engine, felt another surge, and watched the needle on his Mach meter move slowly through the speed of sound. At precisely Mach 1.06 he switched off the motor and gently glided back down to the ground.

In all, the two Bell X-1s made 157 powered and unpowered drops, achieving a maximum speed of Mach 1.45 (957 MPH) and a maximum altitude of 71,902 feet. Both planes were retired in October, 1951.

Supersonic Flight

When the NACA saw how successful the first two X-1 planes were, they immediately ordered Bell to build three more. Completed as the X-1A, the X-1B, and the X-1D (X-1C was never built), they were bought for the purpose of exploring flying conditions above Mach 2, twice the speed of sound, and altitudes above 90,000 feet. Flights began in 1951 and on December 12, 1953, Charles Yeager pushed his X-1A to a speed of Mach 2.44 at 75,000 feet. That represented a speed of 1,650 MPH. When Yeager noticed a slow roll to the left and tried to correct it the plane went out of control. For more than six miles, the tiny plane tumbled toward earth, finally leveling off just 25,000 feet above the ground. More than two years earlier, the X-1D had to be jettisoned from the B-29 carrier plane when an explosion ripped through its fuel tank.

High-speed flight research was a dangerous business. Nobody questioned that. During the 1950s, many records were made as bold pilots pushed speeds faster and faster. The record for the three second generation X-1s had been set by the near fatal flight when Yeager reached Mach 2.44. The second X-1 was rebuilt with a thinner

Beginning in 1951, the developed versions of the X-1 family pushed speed close to Mach 2 and explored many high altitude phenomena.

wing and called the X-1E, although it was not a new plane. Since the first X-1 had been retired to a museum, that left just the four remaining planes to push ahead with essential research work. The need to develop flight research for the coming generation of high-speed jet fighters kept the X-planes in the air as frequently as possible.

By the early 1950s, combat planes were being designed for speeds almost as fast as the X-craft had reached. First of these was the F-100 Super Sabre, the first plane in the world to take off and land under its own power and achieve Mach 1 in level flight. It first flew in May, 1953, when the fastest X-1 had only reached Mach 1.45. Engineers at the NACA were worried. They feared pilots might encounter conditions they had not been taught to expect. The NACA began studies in 1952 of a far reaching program for very high speed flight research. At the heart of it would be a plane capable of speeds up to Mach

Also developed by Bell, the X-2 had a sad history of problems, delays and crashes.

Like all X-series rocket propelled research planes, the X-2 was carried aloft under the belly of a converted B-29 Superfortress, seen here jacked up to allow the plane to be maneuvered snugly underneath.

Satisfactorily in position and attached to its carrier plane, the X-2's undercarriage is raised and the bomber slowly lowered to ground level.

10 and an altitude of 50 miles, the height where space officially began!

Until the Mach 10 plane could be built, research was to continue with the Bell X-2. Ordered by the air force in 1947, this plane had wings swept back from the fuselage. When the first X-1 series had been built, engineers thought a straight wing would be better for supersonic speed. Although not an X-series plane, the navy put swept wings on its Skyrocket and both this and the X-2 competed for the honor of being the first plane through Mach 2. The navy won in November, 1953, although the air force was able to celebrate the fiftieth anniversary of manned flight just a few weeks later with its X-1 flight at Mach 2.44.

The X-2 was built for speeds up to Mach 3. Powered by a 15,000 pound thrust rocket motor, the plane was more than 45 feet long and, at 12 tons, weighed twice as much as the X-1. It was not as successful as its predecessors, however. Unpowered flight tests began in 1952, but the first rocket assisted drop took place more than three years later. One of two planes had been destroyed in an accident and it was April, 1956, before the first supersonic flight could take place with the remaining plane. On September 27, 1956, the X-2 dropped away from its carrier plane and roared to a record Mach 3.2, about 2,094 MPH. Seconds later it went out of control and began a long, tumbling fall to earth, killing the pilot. The speed record would stand for almost four years.

During the first ten years of supersonic flight research, large amounts of recorded data from heavily instrumented X-planes helped ensure astonishing progress in aviation. By the late 1950s, fighter planes capable of Mach 2.3 were coming into service. The air force even had a supersonic bomber that flew at twice the speed of sound. In ten years, military flyers were handling planes nearly three times as fast as their predecessors.

An X-2 is prepared for flight, typical of the missions that carried one plane of this type through Mach 3.2 seconds before it lost control and crashed to the desert floor.

The Edge of
Space

Built to fly at more than Mach 6, these three X-15 research planes represented the peak of rocket propelled hypersonic flight. They were operated under a cooperative program between NASA and the Air Force.

By the late 1950s, jet fighter planes had been developed to the point where there was no reason to make them go faster. Interceptors built to chase after intruding bombers at Mach 2 were flying, and some had already joined air force squadrons. Most notable of these were the F-106 Delta Dagger and the F-104 Starfighter. Both could fly at speeds considerably in excess of Mach 2 and served as air defense fighters. By the early 1960s, attention focused on better handling and maneuverability at lower speeds. Back when high speed flight research was limited to less than Mach 3, however, there

seemed to be a pressing need to build faster X-planes. In 1955, North American Aviation was chosen to build the X-15. It would mark the peak of high speed aerodynamic research in the United States for many years to come.

The X-15 was very different from the tiny, 6 ton, X-1 series or the 12 ton X-2. From the beginning, it was built for *hypersonic* speed based on known conditions up to Mach 3. Unlike its predecessors, which were designed without prior knowledge of conditions they would meet, the X-15 would fly with the benefit of research already conducted at low Mach numbers. Never-

For the first time, a converted B-52 bomber was used to lift a research plane into the sky, from where it was released to begin just a few minutes of rocket flight. Note the escorting chase planes below and behind.

theless, it pioneered new ways of flying and was equipped with systems never before tried out. Also, because it weighed nearly 17 tons, it would be lifted into the air by a specially modified Boeing B-52 four jet bomber.

The X-15 was ready for flight by June, 1959. The oval shaped fuselage was 50 feet long and carried two bulbous *fairings*, one on each side. From these, two thin, *trapezoidal* wings emerged to a span of just 22 feet. Power was to be provided by a single rocket engine delivering 50,000 pounds of thrust for a mere 85 seconds. The rocket ship would have little more than a minute to reach phenomenal speeds hitherto untested. Although earlier intentions had been to give the X-15 a maximum speed of Mach 10, this ambitious goal had long been abandoned in favor of a plane capable of Mach 6. Still, it was a major step ahead of anything else and would provide

valuable data for more than 9 years.

Three X-15 planes were built, and the first made its initial glide flight in June, 1959. The

With a powerful rocket motor, the X-15 was used to explore flight control characteristics at altitudes in excess of fifty miles above the surface of the earth.

Test pilot William McKnight walks away from an X-15 modified with white heat protective material for its record-breaking run to Mach 6.7.

second X-15 made the next flight when test pilot Scott Crossfield flew it to Mach 2.1 (1,393 MPH). In May, 1960, the first X-15 nudged past the record set by the X-2, minutes before it crashed in September, 1956. In March, 1961, the X-15 broke through Mach 4 when it reached a speed of 2,905 MPH. This was followed several flights later by a flight through Mach 5 in June of the same year, and Mach 6 in November. By this time, the third plane had joined the other two and a long series of research flights was under way.

When the X-15 started flying, the height record stood at 87,750 feet, set by the X-2 in 1956. That was exceeded in August, 1960, and eight months later the X-15 reached an altitude of 246,700 feet. Within a period of five months, it had demonstrated design speed and height goals, but there was more to come. In August, 1963, the third X-15 soared to an altitude of 354,200 feet, an all-time record. At this height the plane was kept stable by tiny thrusters in its wings, just like the NASA space shuttle is kept oriented in space by similar thrusters in its nose and tail. Because it had been higher than 50 miles, officially laid down as the line between atmosphere and space, its pilot received astronaut wings! The second X-15 was modified and a record speed run of Mach 6.7 (4,520 MPH) was made by this plane in October, 1967.

Just over a month later the third X-15 plummeted to earth when it re-entered the denser layers of the atmosphere at the wrong altitude. Pilot Michael Adams was killed. He was the only fatality of the entire program. X-15 flights ended in October, 1968, and nothing replaced them. NASA was planning to build a reusable space

shuttle. More than fourteen years later, this winged space-plane would re-enter the atmosphere at Mach 25 (17,500 MPH) and glide back to earth. Of the twelve men who rode the X-15, eight could be officially classed as astronauts. In reality, some were. In 1969 Neil Armstrong became the first man to walk on the moon, and in 1981 Joe Engle was commander of the second shuttle mission.

On some missions special saddle tanks were used to carry additional fuel for the rocket motor in high speed, long duration test flights.

Edwards Air Force Base

Most new planes used by the U.S. Air Force and the U.S. Navy are tested at Edwards Air Force Base, a unique facility north of Los Angeles in California. It lies at the edge of the Mojave Desert spread across several dry lake beds. Edwards is best known as the place where the famous X-series, rocket-propelled research planes have pushed high-speed flight up through Mach 6 and to altitudes above 354,000 feet. These planes have earned a place in history because they are used to test flying machines at speeds and heights no other planes can reach. Because of this, Edwards Air Force Base is famous all over the world, and many test pilots from several countries go there to test their skills.

Carrying names like Rogers, Rosamund, and Mojave, the dry lakes around Edwards are good for flight tests with new planes. Their surface is crusted with salt left behind when shallow seas dried up millions of years ago. Very flat and with a good surface for high-speed landings, the dry lake beds provide the longest runways anywhere. Moreover, tiny cracks that form on the surface due to hot sun are constantly being

Edwards Air Force Base is the home of Air Force flight research and the Dryden Flight Center operated by NASA.

In special test facilities special planes like this highly maneuverable fighter design are first put through their paces. Many of these planes never result in a production order but lead to considerable improvements with more conventional designs.

filled in by sediment. This sediment is left behind when water blown across the surface by high winds evaporates. The same water dissolves salts from the sediment, and in turn the sun dries it to a hard crust, baking the surface. The heaviest aircraft in the world can land easily on this hard bed.

Flight testing came to Rogers dry lake in 1933 when the Army used it for bombing and gunnery practice. Officers and men were housed at the little town of Muroc, which was to become the center for aeronautical research. Before that happened, however, most experimental test flying took place at Wright Field, a heavily populated area outside Dayton, Ohio. When the U.S. Army started testing jets, a less populated area was essential for safety reasons. In 1942 the shift was made to what was now called Muroc Flight Test Base alongside Rogers dry lake. In honor of Capt. Glen W. Edwards, killed in 1948 while flying an experimental bomber, it was renamed Edwards Air Force Base.

Enemy aircraft captured during the Second World War (1939-1945) were test flown at Edwards to discover technical details that might be of use. It was the site for Chuck Yeager's famous flight through Mach 1, which broke the sound barrier for the first time. That event was conducted with the help of the National Advisory Committee for Aeronautics (NACA), the aeronautical research organization for the United States. NACA and the Air Force developed a

In wind tunnels, models of futuristic planes are mounted in movable rigs that can test every possible aspect of the plane's performance at high speed.

Called Hyper III this test model is prepared for an aerial drop after being carried to an altitude of 10,000 feet by a helicopter and will be radio-controlled like a model plane as it glides toward a landing.

research program for rocket propelled planes and formed at Edwards the High-Speed Flight Research Station. In 1959 the NACA was dissolved and replaced by the National Aeronautics and Space Administration (NASA). Seven years later the High-Speed Flight Station was renamed the Hugh L. Dryden Flight Research Center in honor of NASA's first Deputy Administrator.

In 1977, Dryden was the base from where the first shuttle was lifted into the air on the back of a converted Boeing 747 Jumbo Jet airliner and released to glide safety to a perfect landing, proving that the world's first reusable spaceplane would fly.

Today, Dryden is managed by NASA's Ames Research Center, at Moffett Field, California. Over the years its name and the activities it supports have changed many times. There is no longer any work going on with rocket powered planes, and attention is focused now on different shapes of airplanes. In a few years, there will be new rocket-powered research planes. NASA and the air force will begin testing the hypersonic X-30 sometime during the mid-1990s.

The research carried out by the U.S. Air Force at Edwards and by NASA at Dryden has always made use of the latest technology, and aviation has progressed and become safer every year. Surprisingly, there are fewer fatal accidents at Dryden than at any other base, a statistic that reflects the remarkable skills of the test pilots who daily risk their lives to perfect new planes.

Aerospace contractors regularly use the facilities at Edwards and have established their own presence on this exotic desert base.

Riding the Air

Although not originally built as a research plane, the cancelled XB-70 Mach 3 bomber found a home at Edwards Air Force Base as a research plane. It is seen here alongside the modified X-15.

In the twenty years from 1947 to 1967, speed records went from less than 700 MPH to more than 4,200 MPH, a six-fold increase. Fighter planes increased their performance dramatically. Their designers wanted to provide pilots with planes that could reach marauding bombers in a matter of minutes. For their part, engineers designing new bombers were continually pressed by the air force for methods of escaping the fighters. It was assumed that, if the United States had fighters capable of Mach 2.5, then potential enemy forces would soon have the same. The bombers would be vulnerable to attack.

There was one more concern. Anti-aircraft missiles were just being developed. These could reach heights of about 40,000 feet and speeds of Mach 3. To escape both missiles and fighters, a bomber was needed that could fly faster and higher than everything else. In 1954, when NACA design studies were just putting together the specification for the X-15, the air force drew up a specification for its supersonic bomber. It would result in the biggest research plane ever built and in some ways the most futuristic.

Called the XB-70A Valkyrie, it was built by North American Aviation, now Rockwell International. It had to fly as fast as possible and

In its day, the XB-70 was the fastest and highest flying bomber and has never been challenged in performance since its first flight in 1966.

carry a heavy load of bombs more than 5,000 miles at 70,000 feet. Mach 3 was the minimum speed necessary to escape missiles and fighter planes. This posed a very big problem because the bomber would not be able to carry sufficient fuel to fly that fast over several thousand miles. North American came up with a novel solution, one that has never been repeated since.

To make it more efficient as it flew through the air at Mach 3, the plane was shaped underneath in such a way that it would ride on its own shock wave. All planes flying at supersonic speed create shock waves because the air cannot move aside fast enough to make way for them. The result of the shock wave effect can be heard on the ground as a loud bang when the plane flies by. To permit long-duration flight at Mach 3, the XB-70A was designed to behave much like a speed boat on water, which rises up on its keel as it goes faster. This cuts down the boat's resistance. It had the same effect on the Valkyrie.

The bomber was designed to ride on its own shock wave created by the huge box carrying six powerful turbojet engines underneath the wing and main body of this enormous plane.

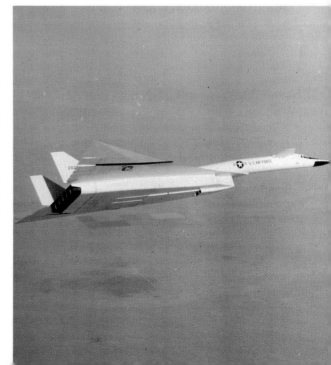

When the XB-70A appeared publicly for the first time in May, 1964, its role as a bomber was already extinct. The Valkyrie had taken nearly seven years to build, and in that period defense planners had decided that the best way to avoid attack was to fly very low rather than high at Mach 3. The Valkyrie was useless at low altitude. The two planes eventually built were turned over the the U.S. Air Force and NASA for research. At this time the United States was conducting research on a supersonic airliner. The Valkyrie was believed to be very useful for this work because it was the only Mach 3 plane of sufficient size.

With a length of almost 197 feet and a wing span of 105 feet, it weighed more than 270 tons fully loaded. It was powered with six jet engines delivering a total thrust of 163,200 pounds, about half the power of the rocket that put the first United States astronaut in orbit. These engines were the loudest jets ever flown, and they consumed enormous quantities of fuel. The outer wing tips were hinged to fold down at Mach 3 to help maintain the proper flow of air over the rear section. Folded like that, they gave the plane a weird appearance, like some enormous aquatic ray.

The Valkyrie first flew in September, 1964, and the first plane was joined by a second in July, 1965. Eleven months later the first Valkyrie was involved in a collision with a Starfighter flown by NASA test pilot Joe Walker. The two planes crashed to the floor of the Mojave desert in California. The remaining XB-70A continued to carry out research until it was retired to a museum in February, 1969, just four months after the last X-15 flight. In all, the Valkyries flew 106 supersonic hours, and the highest speed recorded was Mach 3.08. They were very useful in providing important data about the effects on very large planes of sustained flight at Mach 3.

For very high speed (Mach 3 +) flight the wing tips were designed to hinge down and provide a better flow of air across the tail.

One XB-70 crashed in 1966 but the second continued to carry out valuable flight research until it was retired to a museum at Wright Patterson Air Force Beach at Dayton, Ohio, where it can be seen today.

Lifting Bodies

First of a new generation of Lifting Body research planes designed to explore the handling characteristics of a blended wing-body design, the M2-F2 is seen here at Edwards Air Force Base.

In the late 1950s, NASA designed manned vehicles to carry astronauts into space. They were launched by conventional rockets and returned to earth by falling like a stone until parachutes slowed their descent. The final impact was cushioned by having them fall in water from where naval forces would retrieve them. It was a complicated business and very expensive. Engineers knew it was only a matter of time before spacecraft were built like planes so they could fly back down to a controlled landing on a suitable runway. Conventional airplane wings would not give the space-plane sufficient lift to maneuver over great distances. NASA decided to try another solution.

The one they chose was to blend the body and the wings into a continuously molded shape. Calculations showed that prospects were good for the eventual development of a real space-plane. Before that could become reality, however, tests were necessary to try out these ideas. Constructed of plywood and tubular steel, the first of these "lifting body" designs had no engine and weighed 1,140 pounds. It was towed

by a plane to a height of 10,000 feet from where its pilot brought it to a controlled landing.

Success was rewarded by further research and NASA ordered two different lifting body designs from Northrop. The first, called M2-F2, was flat on top and rounded on the bottom. Called HL-10, the second was exactly the opposite and had more of a delta shape. Both weighed less than five tons, were 22 feet long, and had a 1,000-pound thrust rocket motor. The idea was not to go as fast as possible, but to carefully test subsonic handling characteristics. These planes were carried into the air attached to the wing of a B-52, the same plane used to lift the X-15. From a height of about 45,000 feet, they were released to try out various maneuvers and glide down to a safe landing.

Second of three Lifting Body designs was this HL-10 built like its companion the M2-F2 by Northrop.

94358

The first M2-F2 flight came in July, 1966. Sixteen flights later, in May the following year, pilot Bruce Peterson lost control just before landing and suffered severe facial injuries when his lifting body tumbled end over end down the runway. Film of that crash was used in opening shots of the TV movie, *Six Million Dollar Man.* The tiny plane was rebuilt as the M2-F3, and a third fin was added to the two existing ones. It resumed flight trials in June, 1970, and was retired at the end of 1972. In its original and rebuilt configuration, the M2-F made 43 flights.

Meanwhile, the HL-10 had come and gone. It first flew in December, 1966, and made 37 successful test drops up to its last in July, 1970. It achieved the highest speed of any lifting body, reaching Mach 1.86 in February, 1970, and the highest altitude, when it soared to more than 90,000 feet on the following flight. As with the M2-F, several flights were made without power. These lasted about four minutes, compared with approximately six minutes for a rocket-propelled flight. Landing speeds varied between 160 and 240 MPH.

The HL-10 had a rounded underbody, a flat upper deck and three fins as seen here as the plane prepares to turn on to its runway at Edwards Air Force Base.

Martin-Marietta built this X-24A for the Air Force Lifting Body research program, a design which was subsequently modified by the addition of an elongated nose.

The third lifting body was built for the air force by Martin Marietta. Called the X-24A, it differed from the NASA lifting bodies by having yet another shape and two fins on a wingless body. It was about 24 feet long with a span of 13 feet across the fin tips and weighed 5 tons. This plane made 28 flights between April, 1969, and June, 1971, before it was grounded for modifications. When it appeared again two years later, it had a long pointed nose, extending its length by 13 feet, and a new tip span of 19 feet. Weight had now gone up to more than 6 tons. Called X-24B, it conducted many flight tests before retirement in November, 1975.

Between 1966 and 1975, these strange little planes paved the way for a reusable spacecraft.

Although it looked very different from any of the shapes that flew from Edwards Air Force Base, the NASA shuttle gained much from research conducted by the lifting bodies. One X-24B pilot, Francis R. Scobee, became an astronaut and flew a shuttle mission in 1984. He commanded the ill-fated *Challenger* mission which blew up 73 seconds after launch, in January, 1986.

From left to right, the X-24A, the M2-F2, and the HL-10 are seen together on the desert lake bed runway before retirement in 1975.

Wind Tunnels and Weird Shapes

Many strange shapes in the skies today will become the planes of tomorrow. All new ideas and technical developments must first be tried out in experimental research airplanes. Gone are the days when planes were designed on a drawing board, built in a few weeks, and boldly tried out in the air. Instead, computers and wind tunnels are used extensively to help engineers get the best, and the safest, design. Engineers use models to watch how they behave and to measure simulated flights planned for full-size planes.

Wind tunnels are very important because they provide test conditions without risking a pilot's life. First, calculations are made about the way a particular design will behave in air. Then, a small model is made and to it are attached many different measuring devices. Called sensors, they look at the way air flows over the model's surfaces and how it reacts to various controls and maneuvers. The models can be moved around inside the wind tunnel when it is in full operation, duplicating the motion of a full-size plane.

Some designs are so futuristic they will go

Wind tunnels like this seen at the NASA Langley Research Center are an important part of trying out various plane shapes to get exactly the right configuration before full size models are prepared.

Carried into the air by a converted B-52, this research plane has just been released from its latched position under the shoe of a pylon between the main body of the plane and its inner engines.

through several different changes of shape before the final one is selected. The wind tunnel provides measurements and information which is examined with the help of powerful computers. NASA operates a very big wind tunnel at the Ames Research Center, Moffett Field, California. It is 90 feet wide and 40 feet high, enabling engineers to put full-size planes inside to simulate real flying conditions. Design models of future planes are built for use in this wind tunnel.

In one design, NASA tested a fighter designed to take off and land in very short distances. Planes like this would have advantages because they could use damaged runways rather than divert to another airfield. They could also use special strips hidden by trees and escape attack. Because of the unique design of their engine, which blows some of the exhaust through special slots in the wing, these planes need extensive wind tunnel tests before they can be safely flown. In another design, NASA engineers tested a rocket-boosted space vehicle, simulating high supersonic speeds.

On all test drops chase planes accompany the B-52 monitoring with camera equipment every sequence in the complicated operation of test flying a new vehicle.

When tunnel tests prove computer predictions about favorable shapes, it is time to take them to the air. NASA operates a Boeing B-52 which, since the late 1960s, has been used to test drop many different shapes. Some of the tests take place with pilots and some without. Measurements are clearly a vital part of getting useful information from the drop, so the planes are usually wired with sensitive measuring devices. Some of the information is transmitted to the ground, some goes back to the B-52, and some is recorded on board and recovered later. Of equal importance are the photographs that show how well the test plane responds to different flying conditions. Modified F-104 and T-38 planes are used to take pictures all the time during a drop.

When a plane's shape has been tried out in a wind tunnel, modified according to what the results are, and drop-tested from a carrier plane, a full-size version is built and flown with pilots on board. Some planes go straight from being models in a wind tunnel to full-size flight planes. Typical is the Quiet Short-Haul Aircraft, or QSRA. Part of a joint U.S. Navy/NASA program, the QSRA lands at a slow 75 MPH. This means it can fly on and off aircraft carriers without using special aids to stop it. Flight research of this kind is the most exciting, because test pilots get the chance to try out completely new concepts in flying. Without such research, planes would be a lot less safe, airliners would not be as reliable as they are, and aeronautical progress would slow down.

This NASA Quiet Short-Haul Aircraft (QSRA) is part of a joint U.S. Navy/NASA program aimed at reducing the noise of small transport planes and shortening the run necessary to take off and land, as being demonstrated here on a U.S. Navy carrier.

The QRSA represents one type of flight research which, although less exotic than rocket propelled high speed flight, is an essential part of flight test programs.

Reshaping the Wing

Directly in support of an operational fighter program, NASA and industry helped develop a special wing for this AV-8B vertical take-off plane which gave it added lifting capability and a better operational performance.

The business of making planes more efficient, perform better, or cost less has kept engineers busy since the Wright brothers made the first flight in 1903. Wings have had their fair share of modification. From planes with two or more wings to planes that usually have only one wing, designs have evolved to keep pace with science and technology. There are wings that fold up on navy planes to make more room aboard aircraft carriers and wings that sweep back in flight to give fighters or bombers more maneuverability. There are even wings that, at certain times, play no part in the plane's ability to stay in the air. Such is the wing on the AV-8B.

Built by McDonnell Douglas in the United States and by British Aerospace in England, the AV-8B is a vertical take-off and landing (VTOL) strike fighter. It rises on the thrust of its down facing engine exhausts and can gently lower itself back to the ground. This wing is only used when the plane travels forwards in normal flight. From an original wing developed in England, McDonnell Douglas has made changes which add much greater lift. This allows more weight to be carried, in the form of extra fuel or weapons. Part of the secret comes from a special carbon material used to make the wing. It is lighter, stiffer, and can take more stress than

Called the AD-1, this pivot wing research plane has been tested from research centers in California in an attempt to improve high speed flight performance and wing efficiency which would result in cheaper travel.

the original wing made of aluminum.

In the never-ending search to make planes quieter, especially those operating as commercial airliners, NASA turned to a revolutionary type of new wing design. It was developed at the Ames and Dryden Flight Research Centers in California. Attached to a plane known simply as the AD-1, engineers bolted a rigid wing pivoted in the center where it is attached to the top of the fuselage. Called an "oblique" wing, it can pivot around giving the plane the appearance of a pair of scissors.

For normal flight the wing is in the conventional position. It enables the plane to fly with

HiMAT (highly maneuverable aircraft technology) was built by Rockwell for unmanned tests dropped from the wing of a B-52.

less engine power, making it much quieter to operate. For high speed flight the wing is pivoted so that one side points toward the nose and the other side toward the tail. Calculations show that a transport plane with a wing of this type flying at 1,000 MPH would be twice as efficient as one using a conventional wing. This would significantly reduce costs and cut operating expenses.

In a special program called HiMAT, for Highly Maneuverable Aircraft Technology, NASA and the U.S. Air Force flew a unique plane. It was built by Rockwell and had special design features to test new ways of making fighters more agile. It was not manned by a pilot but controlled by an operator in a cockpit on the ground. Carried into the air by a B-52, HiMAT began flying in 1979. Three years later it started supersonic flight trials and eventually reached a speed of Mach 1.4 at 40,000 feet.

The HiMAT plane has a second, smaller wing ahead of its main wing. This is called a *canard*

Incorporating several new design trends, HiMAT was flown like a model plane with an operator on the ground sending radio signals to control flightpath.

Planes like this have produced a new generation of highly maneuverable combat fighters and set trends in designs and wing layout that will last well into the early years of the next century.

from the French word for duck. Many planes have flown with canards, but this particular design is thought to help fighters improve their maneuverability. The HiMAT plane can make very tight turns at supersonic speeds and is much more agile than any fighter in operational use today. Both NASA and the air force have spent much time examining this design and studying the flight results to come up with an experimental fighter built to carry a pilot.

There is no end to the amount of research under way at NASA and in the military forces to improve airplanes, develop new materials, and provide cheaper and better means of transport. Engineers and designers apply all forms of technology to their tasks. As computers get more advanced, they too are helping engineers redesign the wing.

X-29

In an attempt to provide a very agile fighter, Grumman was chosen to build the X-29 forward swept wing research plane.

The search for agile and more maneuverable fighter planes is a continual one. While nature seems to have set limits on just how fast a plane can be made to twist and turn in the air, humans have made many attempts to stretch those limits or push through them altogether. Theirs is important research, because success in gaining control of the air is a significant part of defense. Powerful engines and the use of computers to design better shapes for fighters reached a peak in the 1970s.

Many different technologies have been tried out in the attempt to improve performance. Fighters have been built with different types of wing, tail, and fuselage arrangements, all to improve handling. Several separate developments

in the 1980s produced the means by which a real breakthrough could be achieved. It is based on very large high-speed computers, new "composite" materials, and miniature electronics tied to compact computers capable of surviving high levels of stress. On their own, none of these would have produced the completely new type of plane now being tested.

For high speed, most planes have swept wings. This is a better shape for pushing through the atmosphere with the least resistance. Airplane designers call this *drag*. The less drag, compared to the lift generated by the wings, the better the plane will fly. One problem still remains, however. As the plane pushes its way through the atmosphere, air first reaches the wing at the

most forward point. This is the place where the wing joins the fuselage, or body, of the plane. It then flows back along the wing and out toward the tips. To control and adjust its attitude, the plane has flaps called *ailerons* which are moved by a control in the cockpit to make the plane turn left or right. By the time the flow of air reaches the ailerons it is weaker and less effective.

In an effort to correct this problem, engineers suggested a plane with wings swept forward instead of back. In that way, air first reaches the

Part of the main body of this small plane is seen here under assembly at Grumman's factory in Bethpage, Long Island, New York.

The real secret of the X-29's forward swept wing is that it is not made of steel but a much stronger composite material bonded from several artificial compounds specially prepared for their strength and very light weight.

wing tips, then flows back and in toward the fuselage. This means that the strongest flow goes over the ailerons, enabling the aircraft's controls to bite on a stronger flow of air. A plane with forward-swept wings can turn more quickly, because its controls are more effective. Very powerful computers worked out all the details, and in 1981, Grumman was selected to build a plane like this.

The X-29, as it is called is made possible because of composite materials. Metals like aluminum would snap under tremendous stress, but composites are made up from several different artificial materials bonded together to make a strong compound from which parts for planes can be made. If made from steel and metal alloys like ordinary fighters, the X-29 would snap apart because the forces it encounters are much greater than those of operational planes today.

To help it maneuver crisply, the X-29 has two forward canard wings, which also perform better than if they were in front of a swept-back wing. Canards have advantages for some planes, but they do create disturbances in the air as it flows back across the surface of the wing. This further reduces the effect of the ailerons, because control surfaces need smooth, not disturbed, air. With the X-29 there are two separate streams of air. One goes straight to the wing tips and back along the ailerons, while the other comes straight back off the small canards. Neither one is affected by the other.

The final problem posed by the forward-swept

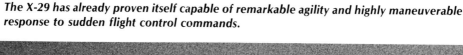

The X-29 has already proven itself capable of remarkable agility and highly maneuverable response to sudden flight control commands.

The X-29 research program will continue to the end of the 1980s and lessons learned from this exciting research program will be one of the requirements the Air Force will lay down for a new 1990s fighter.

wing design is that the plane is very unstable, which is the price paid for its high maneuverability. With miniaturized electronics coupled to a compact computer, the pilot would never be able to keep control of the plane. The ailerons flex and flutter up to 40 times a second, just to keep the plane level. When the pilot takes control and flies the X-29, he is really just controling where it goes. The computer keeps it balanced.

Hypersonic Planes

The last major high-speed research plane built in the United States was the X-15. Capable of Mach 6, it helped pave the way for the NASA shuttle and high-performance planes of the future. Although the shuttle re-enters earth's atmosphere at Mach 25, or about 17,500 MPH, it is built to use friction with the air to slow it down. It does not continually fly in the atmosphere at that speed but uses the air to reduce speed for landing. Many people believe that the United States should build another research plane like

Future planes traveling at very high speeds will probably use ramjet engines scooping up air as they go and operating like a rocket engine at the fringe of the atmosphere.

the X-15, but with much greater performance.

The United States plans to build another research plane for high Mach flight and has given it the designation X-30. Developed by NASA and the Defense Department, this hypersonic plane will pioneer a completely new form of transportation. It will not fly before 1993, and when it does it will be purely experimental. It will be made of unusual materials, exotic types of metal and plastic composites much stronger than steel. The X-30 will also test a completely new type of engine called the *ramjet*.

In conventional jet engines, air is taken in at the front, compressed, and burned before it is fed out the back to provide thrust. These engines operate best from subsonic speeds up to about Mach 3. A ramjet engine takes over at Mach 3 and performs well up to about Mach 15. It works because of the enormous pressure that builds up inside the engine as the plane literally scoops up the atmosphere. Between Mach 15 and Mach 25, which is also the speed needed to stay in orbit, rocket engines are best. These carry their own oxygen in special tanks. Some people think there is an alternative to rocket engines.

One of these is called the *scramjet* engine, and the X-30 will test this also. In a scramjet engine, combustion takes place with gases which are themselves traveling at supersonic speeds. In a ramjet, the air is slowed to subsonic speed for combustion. Nobody has tested scramjets in flight. Several test projects in wind tunnels have shown them to be efficient up to Mach 7, the limit of the tunnel. What engineers now need to know is whether a scramjet-engined aerospace plane can use this form of propulsion to achieve orbital speed.

The X-30 will be a research tool for two different types of planes. It will help develop a

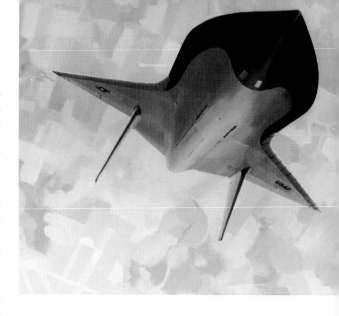

In a cooperative venture between NASA and the Department of Defense, engineers are designing a research plane called the X-30 which will take over where the X-15 left off, exploring flight conditions up to Mach 15.

This Lockheed design for a hypersonic plane would be capable of Mach 5 at an altitude of 100,000 feet and could be used for reconnaissance.

Research on future aerospace vehicles may result in an airliner capable of carrying passengers across great distances at speeds greater than Mach 5.

replacement for the space shuttle, perhaps one that takes off from a runway and flies all the way into orbit without the need of additional rocket motors. This space-plane will have military duties also. It will be capable of flying right around the world on missions to gather pictures and information without being shot down and it will deliver satellites to orbit.

The X-30 will also help prepare the way for a hypersonic airliner, which could fly from Los Angeles to Tokyo, Japan, in just a few hours. Cruising at Mach 5, it would carry up to 350 passengers at 70,000 feet. Scientists believe they know enough already to predict that such a plane is possible by the year 2000. Engineers need to test several new methods of propulsion,

and the X-30 program will provide information about materials and sustained flight at Mach 5. By this time the space-plane will not be far behind, and the day is not far off when passengers flying at more than 3,000 MPH across the Pacific Ocean look out their windows to see a scramjet dart high above them on its way into orbit.

Nobody knows what the X-30 will look like. Design details have yet to be completed. Engineers are busy working out all the characteristics of the plane, and it will soon begin to take shape. By the time people celebrate the 100th anniversary of the first powered flight in the year 2003, flight to the moon may be the next talking point.

Another variation resulting from work on the X-30 may be a space plane capable of taking people and cargo routinely into space and returning to land on a conventional runway. Such a vehicle might be developed from this hypersonic airliner capable of traveling from Los Angeles to Tokyo, Japan, in just over two hours.

ABBREVIATIONS

HiMAT   Highly Maneuverable Aircraft Technology

NACA   National Advisory Committee for Aeronautics

NASA   National Aeronautics and Space Administration

QSRA   Quiet Short-Haul Aircraft

VTOL   Vertical Take-Off and Landing

GLOSSARY

Ailerons   A flap hinged to the trailing edge of an airplane wing to provide lateral control, as in a bank to the left or the right or in a roll.

Canard   From the French word for "duck," an airplane that has small wings forward of the main wings.

Drag   Literally, any obstacle to progress. When talking about airplanes, drag is the force that acts on an airplane in a horizontal (called longitudinal) direction, such as air trying to slow the forward motion of the plane.

Fairing   The smoothing of two angular surfaces to provide a blended contour between the two.

Hypersonic   A speed usually regarded as greater than five times the speed of sound, which is 760 MPH at sea level, reducing to 660 MPH at 36,000 feet or above. The speed of sound is rated to a Mach number, Mach 5 being five times the speed of sound (3,800 MPH at sea level or 3,300 MPH at 36,000 feet).

Mach   Mach 1, or unity, is the speed of sound: 760 MPH at sea level, decreasing to 660 MPH at a height of 36,000 feet. Mach 2.2 is equivalent to a speed of 1,672 MPH at sea level or 1,452 MPH above 36,000 feet.

Ramjet   A jet engine designed to operate with enormous pressures of air literally rammed in at the front as the airplane moves in a forward direction at very high speed.

Scramjet   Essentially the same as a ramjet, but one in which the air entering the inlet is already supersonic.

Supersonic   Speeds higher than the speed of sound, which is about 760 MPH at sea level, slowly decreasing to about 660 MPH at an altitude of 36,000 feet and above.

Trapezoidal A quadrilateral shape having neither pair of sides parallel. In the context of an airplane wing, a shape without parallel lines on either tip, wing root, leading, or trailing edges.

INDEX

Page references in *italics* indicate photographs or illustrations.